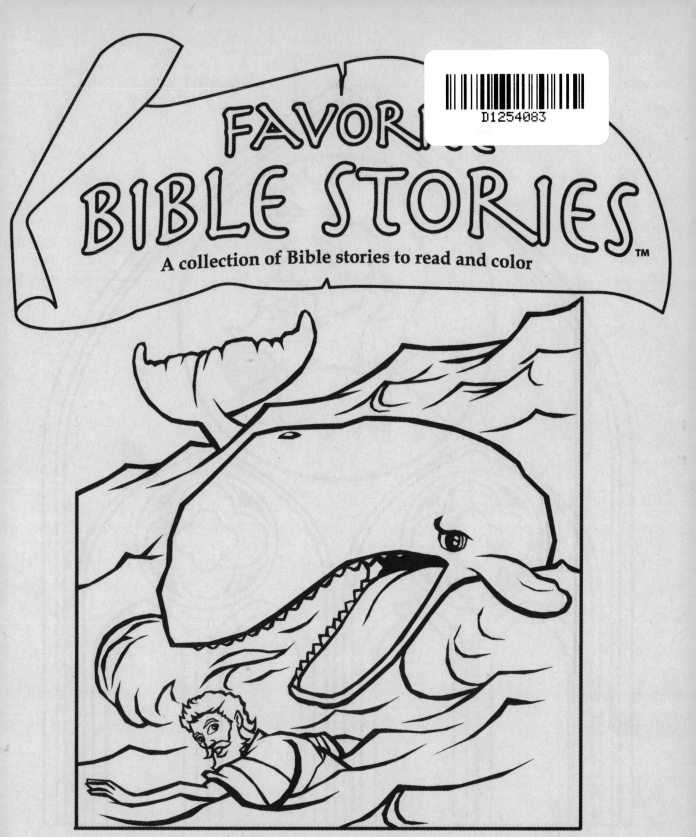

FAVORITE BIBLE STORIES™

A collection of Bible stories to read and color

 KAPPA Books
A Division of KAPPA Graphics, L.P.

Visit us at www.kappapublishing.com/kappabooks

Jonah in the Fish

Jonah lived a simple life by himself in the country a very long time ago.

One day when Jonah prayed, God spoke to him and told Jonah
to go to the city of Nineveh to tell the King and the people
that God was very angry with them.

Jonah was afraid. Why would the King of a great city listen to him? Instead he got on a boat that was sailing away from Nineveh.

But a great storm came upon the ship and all the sailors were very frightened.

Everyone except Jonah prayed for help, but the storm got
worse. Finally, Jonah told them that God was angry with him
for disobeying.

The sailors asked God to forgive them and threw Jonah over the
side of the boat into the sea.

A giant fish opened its mouth and swallowed Jonah as the storm stopped.

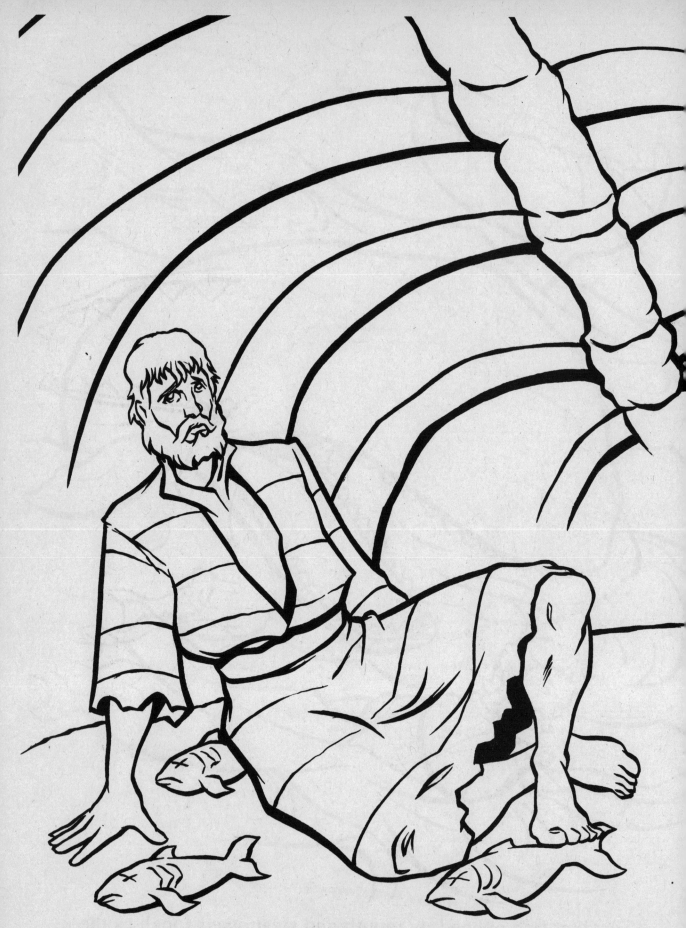

Jonah was in the fish's belly for three days and nights, and was very frightened.

Finally Jonah prayed for God to forgive him and promised to do what God wanted him to.

The fish finally opened its mouth and Jonah stepped onto dry
land near the city of Nineveh.

Jonah walked through the gates and into the great city yelling
"Repent or God will destroy this city in forty days!"

For forty days, Jonah delivered God's message. Then he sat on a hill outside the city and waited for God to destroy it.

The King and all his people were very frightened, and they all prayed to God for forgiveness for their sins. God knew they meant it, and forgave them.

Jonah was angry that God didn't destroy the city. He thought it
made him look like a liar, or a false prophet, so he ran away
from the city.

During the night, God made a little gourd plant beside Jonah grow very large. When he awoke, Jonah sat in the shade of the plant and rested all day, eating the fruit.

But the next morning, the plant had withered and died. Jonah
lay in the burning sun, crying over the dead plant.

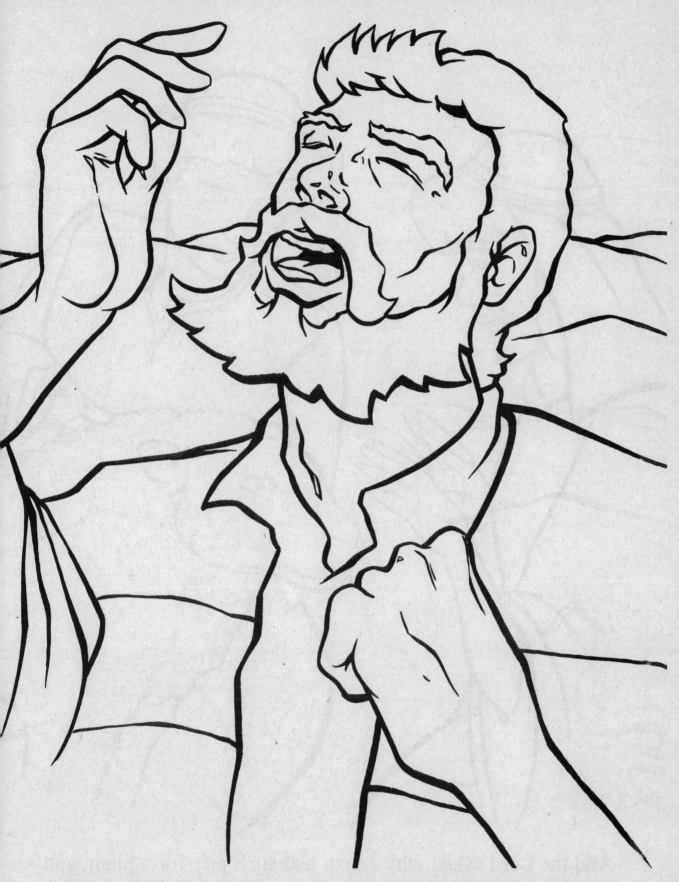

Jonah prayed and asked why God had destroyed the plant
and not him?

And the Lord asked why Jonah had such pity for a plant, and yet none for the city of Nineveh, with its thousands of innocent children and animals.

Jonah thanked God for all His mercy and asked the Lord for
forgiveness, and never questioned God's will again.

Daniel Among the Lions

Daniel was born in Jerusalem, but was taken away as a prisoner when the King of Babylon's army conquered the city.

King Nebuchadnezzar dreamed of terrible things, and Daniel was chosen to be his advisor because of his ability to understand dreams.

One night, the King dreamed about a tree that was so high it reached up to heaven, but the angels talked of cutting it down.

Daniel explained that the tree was the King, and if he didn't stop thinking that he was as powerful as God, he would lose his kingdom.

Nebuchadnezzar didn't believe Daniel and laughed at him, so
God made the King very sick and he never ruled again.

The King's son Belshazzar became the new ruler of Babylon,
and threw a great party to celebrate.

While they ate, a giant hand appeared and wrote some words in the stone wall. No one could read the words so the King sent for Daniel. The words read, "Mene, Mene, Tekel, Parsin."

Daniel told Belshazzar that he had insulted God. The words said that God was angry and the kingdom would be divided and given to the King's enemies.

Later that same night, while the feast was still going, the
Persian army attacked and conquered Babylon.

Darius became the new King. He liked Daniel so much that he
put Daniel in charge of the newly conquered land and all other
administrators.

The other Princes didn't like this, so they decided to get rid of
Daniel. They made a new law that said it was against the law
to pray to any man or god other than King Darius.

Daniel loved God very much and prayed three times a day.
The next time he prayed, the Princes had Daniel arrested.

Daniel was put into a cave of hungry lions to be eaten, which is how the Persians punished their criminals. A giant stone was placed to block the door so Daniel could not escape.

The King was upset and could not sleep all night. Even though the Persians worshiped statues of false gods, Darius prayed to Daniel's God to save his friend's life.

In the morning, the King and Princes watched as the stone was
moved away from the cave door.

Inside, they saw Daniel sitting calmly with the lions, unharmed.
He told Darius that God had protected him.

King Darius was so happy that he ordered everyone in his kingdom to worship Daniel's God because he was the real, true God.

The Strength
of Samson

After Moses led the children of Israel to the Promised Land,
they lived among the other people already there. One group
was the Philistines, who were mighty warriors.

An angel of God visited a pregnant Israelite. He said that her son would help to free the Israelites from the Philistines, but he must never drink wine and never cut his hair.

The child was named Samson, and he was very strong because be had the strength of God in him. Once, he was attacked by a lion, and killed it with his bare hands.

Samson married a Philistine woman, even though her people treated him badly. She was not a good wife, and her friends made fun of Samson.

Samson asked a riddle at his wedding. If nobody could answer,
Samson would get new clothes from each of the thirty guests.
If he lost, he must give them new clothes.

Samson was angry, when his wife told a guest the answer to the riddle. In his anger, he set fire to fields of grain belonging to the Philistines.

Now the Philistines were angry, and one thousand of them attacked Samson. He had no weapon, so he picked up the jawbone of a donkey from the field and beat them all with it.

Samson was now the Israelite's champion, and he led them for twenty years.

One night the men in the town of Gaza waited outside the city
gates to capture him, but Samson ripped the gates down and
carried them away, and the men ran away.

Samson fell very much in love with another Philistine woman named Delilah. She was very beautiful, but she was also cunning and treacherous and wanted to hurt Samson.

The Philistines promised Delilah a lot of money if she could discover the secret of Samson's strength so that he could be captured.

Every night Delilah asked Samson what his secret was, and every night he teased and gave her a false answer.

Finally Delilah was very angry. She said he did not love her, and cried and cried until Samson felt bad. He told her that the strength of God was his as long as his hair was not cut.

That night while Samson slept, Delilah cut off all Samson's hair and called the Philistine guards. They easily captured him, because he was now as weak as any other man.

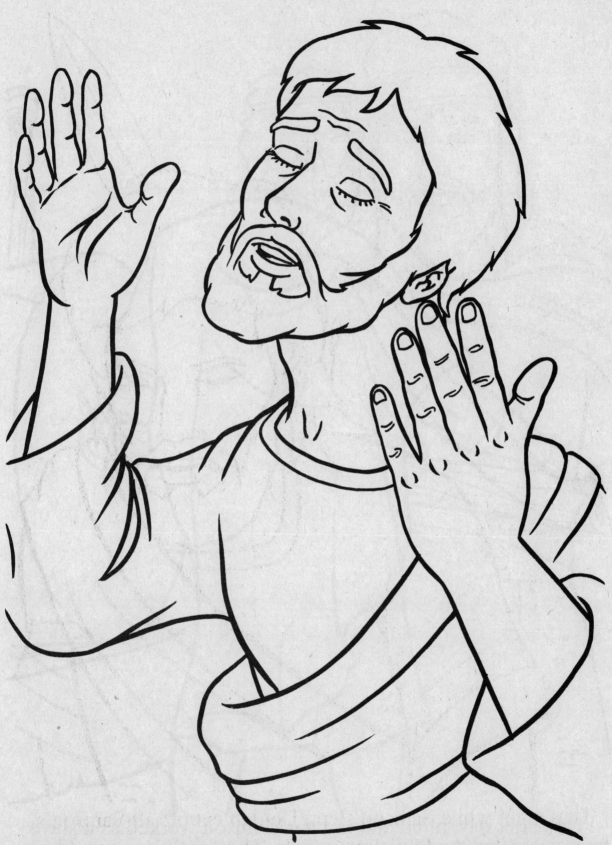

Delilah received her money. The Philistines burned Samson
eyes out and chained him to the wheel of a grist mill like an ox.

Day after day, blind and in pain, Samson worked as a slave turning the great stone to grind grain for the Philistines. And all the while his hair was growing back, but he did not know it.

The Philistines had a feast to celebrate the capture of their
enemy Samson. Thousands of them celebrated in their temple,
praying to the statutes of their Gods.

"Send Samson out to entertain us," they shouted. Samson was led into the temple where the Philistines laughed at him and mocked the blind man.

Samson asked the slave boy who led him around to lean him against the pillars that supported the temple for a few moment to rest.

Samson placed one hand on each pillar and prayed for God to give him strength just one more time. He pushed with all his might. The pillars moved and then tumbled over.

The roof caved in, killing everyone in the temple, including
Samson. But the Philistines and their rulers had all died, and
the Israelites' enemies were vanquished.

God's Promise to Abraham

After the Great Flood, Noah's family prospered and spread across the world. Eventually, they began to forget about God, but the Lord had no wish to destroy them all again.

Instead, God decided to reward the faithful, Abraham. The shepherd was a descendent of Noah's son Shem and was true to God, despite all the evil people around him.

God told Abraham to take his family and go to the land of
Canaan. Abraham gathered his wife, Sarah, his nephew, Lot,
their servants and animals and did as God had told him.

As Abraham looked across the River Jordan into the rich green pastures of Canaan, God promised Abraham that all he saw would someday belong to his descendants.

But God told them a famine was coming, so Abraham and his family traveled into Egypt where there was food. There, Abraham's wife Sarah became close to the Pharaoh.

Abraham and Sarah were very wealthy, but they were sad because they had no children. Abraham was nearly a hundred years old now, and Sarah was ninety.

Soon after, three strangers came to visit and one told Abraham
they would come back again in a year to visit Abraham and
Sarah's newborn son.

Sarah, who was cooking food in the tent heard this and laughed to herself, thinking that she was too old to bear children. One stranger asked her if anything was impossible for God.

The visitors revealed that they were angels from Heaven. One told Abraham that Sarah really would have a son, and as many descendants as there were stars in the sky.

God remembered his promise, and the next year Sarah had a baby boy. He was named Isaac. His parents loved him very much, and he made them happy in their old age.

But God was worried that Abraham loved his son more than he loved God, so He told Abraham to bring his son to a mountain and make a sacrifice of him.

Abraham was very sad, but he always obeyed God. In those days, men made a sacrifice by offering something important of theirs to God: a shepherd's finest animal, or a farmer's best grain.

Abraham told his son how much he loved him, but that God had demanded Isaac as a sacrifice. He kissed the boy and raised his knife to kill his beloved son.

But an angel stopped Abraham, because now God knew that Abraham loved Him more than anything in the world.

Joseph the Dreamer of Dreams

Jacob had twelve sons. His favorite was Joseph, who reminded Jacob of his dead wife. He gave Joseph a beautiful coat woven of many colors. Joseph's brothers were very jealous.

The more Jacob loved Joseph, the more his brothers hated him.
Once Joseph dreamt that he and his brothers were harvesting
wheat in the fields, and their sheaves bowed down to his.

Another time, he dreamed that the sun, moon and stars all
bowed to him. When Joseph told his dreams to his brothers,
they hated him even more for thinking he was better than them.

His brothers were so angry, they beat Joseph, stripped off his fancy coat and pushed him into a dry well.

They planned to kill Joseph, but instead sold their brother into slavery to some merchants going to Egypt, for twenty pieces of silver.

The brothers put blood on Joseph's coat and told their father that he had been killed by a wild animal. Jacob was upset and mourned for his favorite son for many years.

Joseph was sold as a slave to a man named Potiphar, the
captain of Pharaoh's guards in Egypt. Everything Joseph did
was successful, and he was soon Potiphar's best servant.

But Potiphar's wife became angry with Joseph. She told her husband lies about their slave, and Joseph was put into prison for two long years.

One night, the Pharaoh or King of Egypt, had a dream. None of his wise men knew what it meant. A guard remembered the prisoner who interpreted dreams and sent for Joseph.

Pharaoh told Joseph his dream: Seven fat cows were grazing in the fields, and seven thin cows came and ate them up, but the skinny cows stayed thin.

Joseph told Pharaoh the dream was a message from God. There would be seven years of good crops, followed by seven years of famine. Egypt should store up food for the lean years.

Pharaoh put Joseph in care of the food for Egypt, so there would be food in the bad years. Joseph became Prince of Egypt, and only Pharaoh was more powerful.

Joseph stored up grain and food for seven years, and when the
famine arrived, people came from all over to buy food from
him in Egypt, including his brothers.

They did not recognize their brother as they bowed to the Prince of Egypt. Joseph told them he would not sell them any food until they brought their youngest brother Benjamin to Egypt.

Benjamin was Joseph's favorite brother. He told the others that they could have all the food they wanted if Benjamin stayed in Egypt as his slave.

But Joseph's brothers were sad. One begged to stay in Benjamin's place. He explained that their father still grieved for the loss of another son. "He will die if he loses Benjamin too!"

Joseph began to cry and told them he was their brother. They were afraid, but he told them it had been God's plan so they would have food during the famine.

Joseph sent his brothers to bring their father and all their
families back to Egypt. Joseph went in his chariot to meet them
and his father by the border of Egypt in the land of Goshen.

Joseph gave them rich lands there, where the tribes of Israel lived and prospered during the famine and for many more years.